Empath

----- ❧ ❧ -----

How to survive as an empath and embrace your powerful gift as a highly sensitive people.

Wallace Foulds

practitioner in order to ensure you are both able and healthy enough to participate in this program.

Foreword

You've got a gift - empathy. Now, learn how to use it, harness it, and employ it effectively to truly become an empath.

Empathy is one of the softer forces in both communication and social sciences that is both hard to quantify, identify, or feel, and when used effectively, barely noticed - which is where its strength lies.

An empath does not wish to use force, threats, intimidation, or negativity to overcome problems in human communication and social situations.

Instead, an empath employs all the social norms, cues, signals, and empathy with a good dose of common sense to deliver a desirable, harmonious outcome. Life isn't a zero sum game for empaths, a best outcome for everyone is the aim.

- Understand what empathy is, and is not, as well as its power to change lives and social situations for better or worse.

- Identify - Who is an empath? What is an empath? What is empathy? Can I train myself to become more empathetic?

- Assess - Where do my skills lie? What are my strengths as an empath? Am I suited to become an empath? Who are reliable and proficient empaths in my social circles? Where do I fit in best as an empath?

Hone - Understanding your limitations, overcoming your areas of weakness, identifying actors in your social circle who prevent you from becoming an empath, going beyond in new social situations and using your empath skills.

Being an empath does not come naturally, but with enough effort, observation, inflection and practice - it is possible for all. Harness your natural power today through practice, and the good things in life will fall into your lap.

Table of Contents

Chapter 1:

Identify

To begin to understand who an empath is, we must begin to delve into what being an empath means. Unlike a functional job role, being an empath combines social and psychological sciences to harness both skills and functions in synergy with empathy within a person, in relation to the rest of society.

Plainly speaking, being an empath isn't something you can actively train for in a class, or gain just by reading this book. You need to read this book, understand yourself, observe others, learn, adapt it to your social situation(s), and hone your skills. After which, you might gain a limited skill-set, to employ in your daily life.

Remember - empathy is simply the ability to understand how other people feel. Not to feel sorry for them, not to show care, but plainly to understand how they feel. In other words, the ability to put yourselves in their shoes.

Some people are naturally more empathetic than others, naturally, due to various factors such as culture, socio-economic status, and life experiences. However, for most, empathy is a natural human skill that just needs to be put into practice and heightened. In short- you need to be constantly self-aware, and self-reflective.

This can be tiring, but ultimately, a deeper connection with various people and an understanding of how the world functions emotionally will lead to a more fulfilling life.

The Myers Briggs Test

Using the Myers Briggs test as a general indicator may not necessarily be the best to evaluate potential candidates for a job interview, but answered honestly, the Myers Briggs test can be used as a baseline to establish how empathetic you may be.

The Myers Briggs test, briefly, has four categories to grade someone in.

For example: I S F P or E N T J

The first letter can be I, or E, indicating introversion or extroversion.

The second, S, or N, indicating sensing, or intuition

The third, T, or F, indicating thinking or feeling

The fourth, P, or J, Judging, or Perceiving.

The explanations can be found here briefly:

The first criterion, Extraversion – Introversion, represents where the person derives their energy from. Introversion signifies the person's need for space, and alone time to recharge from social situations. Extraversion signifies the person's need to be in company of others, to interact, and communicate to recharge, and gain energy.

The second criterion, Sensing – Intuition, represents the method by which someone perceives information. Sensing indicates that a person tends to focus on the present and on concrete information gained from their senses. Sensing prefers to receive data primarily from the five senses. Intuitions indicates a tendency to focus on the future, with a view toward patterns and possibilities. These people prefer to receive data from the subconscious, or seeing relationships via insights.

The third criterion, Thinking – Feeling, represents how a person processes information. Thinking means that a person makes a decision mainly through logic. Feeling means that, as a rule, he or she makes a decision based on emotion, i.e. based on what they feel they should do.

The fourth criterion, Judging – Perceiving, reflects how a person implements the information he or she has processed. Judging means that a person organizes all of his life events and, as a rule, sticks to his plans. Perceiving means that he or she is inclined to improvise and explore alternative options.

As such, there are 16 possible types of personality types possible.

Empathetic types in MBTI

Before we begin - an important thing to keep in mind is NOT to mix up empathy with caring. Empathy, is the ability to understand and relate to how others feel. Caring, is the actions taken to show care and concern for an individual.

E.g.,

Empathy - Your dog died. Mine died 2 weeks ago. I may understand how you feel, but I don't care.

Empath

Sympathy - Your dog died. Mine died 2 weeks ago. I don't understand how you feel, but I'm sorry your dog died. Have a cupcake I made that looks like your dog.

Introversion VS Extraversion -being an introvert does not naturally mean that you are not empathetic, neither are extroverts empathetic either. Only in relation to the other character dimensions do we see more probabilities.

ENFJs and INFJs, by far are the most empathetic individuals by merit of their usage of both intuition as well as feeling. Their intuition (N) allows them to garner insights as to why people may feel a certain way, their feeling (F), to gather information on emotionally charged situations, or understand emotions in social situations, and lastly, judging (J) allows them to take action and listen, as well as empathize with another person.

ENFPs, as well as INFPs, also have a propensity towards empathy, but in a more caring nature. The key part of INFP and ENFP's that allow them to utilize empathy is the ability to imagine. While not always accurate, imagining yourself in someone else's shoes is a good way to build up a set of skills that lead to being a competent and capable empath.

ENTJs as well as INTJs, may not be as competent as other personality types in empathy, due to their logical, goal oriented behavior, but, with practice and guidance, empathy can definitely be built as a part of character development in all MBTI personality types.

Am I not suited to become an empath?

Empaths are not constrained by personality types. The MBTI types we have covered in the previous section are a baseline, and further reading is recommended to understand yourself and recognize obstacles to becoming a competent empath.

For example - introversion(I) may lead to not wanting to interact, or not having the energy to pay attention to social situations, cues and other social clues as part of building a profile of someone so you can empathize with someone.

Extroversion (E) on the other hand, may lead to a need for validation, or socializing before identifying certain social situations, cues and other social clues as part of building a profile of someone so you can empathize with someone.

Perception - may lead to going with the flow, and not asking certain questions to probe deeper into the individual you aim to empathize with.

Judgement, may lead to asking leading questions, or forming a judgement of a person's situation before a complete picture is revealed. Or, asking questions that already reinforce self-beliefs to form an image of a pre-conceived notion of an individual.

Empaths: Who are they?

Empaths, are people with a set of skills, coupled with the ability to empathize with others to achieve the most favorable outcome, be it for themselves, or others.

Keep in mind - that the fine line between being an empath and a sociopath is a fine one. Empaths use their skills and ability to empathize with others ethically. Sociopaths use their skills and ability to empathize to manipulate others for a self-serving outcome.

Empath

Just remember that the skills taught here, while not manipulative in nature, can cause harm, and caution is needed, as well as self-awareness and reflection of your own moral beliefs and values as to what is right, and wrong.

Professional empaths include: Counsellors, trainers, effective salesmen, team leaders with a good relationship level with their teammates, as well as politicians.

Notice anything? I didn't include engineers, researchers, scientists, policemen, or most authority figures.

While this is a pattern in careers - I'll tell you what the core of it all is. Relationships and power.

Empathy and Related factors

Relationships

As an empath - the number and strength of relationships with others are a core component in your ability to exercise empathy and connect socially with others. The more relationships you have, as well how deep they feel for the other party involved in one with you, be it social, romantic, or professional, or familial, sharpens and hones your ability to empathize and communicate effectively.

Social relationships involves not just friends, but also acquaintances and people you know in passing. These include your neighbors, people you talk to at the supermarket, the old man feeding pigeons in the park you say hello to everytime you pass him while walking your dog, and so on. Most of these relationships are superficial in nature, and do not require much effort to maintain, as there is not much complexity to them.

However, from all social relationships come the opportunity for other forms of relationships.

Familial relationships, are those that comprise of family. While the concept of what defines a family, as contrasted by the traditional family nucleus in western culture, as compared to other forms of extended family, or people living in non-traditional family environments, e.g. kibbutzes or communes.

These relationships are a first form of practice and contact for empaths, however, are difficult to master and use empath skills effectively due to personal attachment to the situation at hand, and most empaths may not have had enough practice with their skills to handle more complex family issues.

Professional relationships are those that you have between two or more people that involve getting a task done, in the most common occurrence is immediate colleagues working together on a project. People in the same workplace whom you don't work with - they fall under social relationships. Usually, these relationships may range from shallow to deep, dependent on the people, but are constrained to a certain environment, or aspect, e.g. the office.

Romantic relationships are between two or more people who have an attraction to one another, and may share more experiences and time as well as energy maintaining the relationship towards each other. These relationships are great for empaths to practice on, but keep in mind that personal attachment as well as involvement may hinder or complicate practicing empath skills.

Empaths, with enough time and energy, generally tend to have happier, more fulfilling relationships with others as well as genuine friendships. By genuine friendships, I mean friendships where both friends have a deeper connection with each other due to common (imagined or real) factors; which lead to a stronger bond.

Power

There are briefly, five types of power. Legitimate, coercive, referential, reward, and expert.

As an empath, you want to leverage on two particular types, and avoid one.

Legitimate - this type of power is conferred on by titles, and positions of power bestowed upon you by a higher authority. Sounds complex?

Simply put, if you are a chairperson of a hobby club, with no ability to punish anyone, or reward anyone, you have legitimate power, as you have been elected.

Coercive - this type of power is good to have but in the context of being an empath, should not be used, as it is not the type you want. Coercive power is simply the power to punish, and will others to do your bidding via means of fear of punishment.

For example - as the manager of a small company, you have coercive power over the other workers, as you have the ability to dock their pay, fire them, or scold them (humiliation).

Referential - This type of power is referred to as 'soft power'. Simply because this is the type of power that belies respect due to various factors, such as age, in certain cultures, past experience of hardship (the person has experience but no skill), love for what the person stands for as a symbol, or other intangible values. Empaths should aim to have this kind of power the most.

E.g. - Celebrities are usually more loved if they have contributed to charitable causes, as are wise old men, for what they represent - kindness and 'good' usage of fame and wealth, and wisdom from old age respectively.

Expert - Expert power is simply power derived from the capacity and usage of specialized or certain knowledge. Your college professor has expert power, or so does an experienced old fisherman, depending on the context. The college professor is adept at biology, and has expert power over that subject in the university, but he does not have expert power while sailing, which the fisherman does from his experience. Conversely, the fisherman does not have expert power in the university.

Empaths should also strive towards this kind of power, but not wield it bluntly through assuming they know everything, or having preconceived notions of social situations.

Reward - Reward power is simply the power to reward people for doing what you want them to do. This form of power, while useful, may not be as relevant to empaths, it can complement, but it should never be used as the main cornerstone in any empath strategy.

A form of reward power - would be that of the manager who has the ability to give out bonuses. The employees want bonuses, so they will do the bidding of the manager in order to acquire said bonuses. That is reward power.

Cultural Norms and Practices

Certain cultures prioritize conformity, others individualism, and there are other dimensions as well, that affect a person's ingrained personal beliefs that stem from culture, and are reinforced by society's expectations of acceptable behavior within that culture.

There are several dimensions to culture but we will touch on a few that are more relevant to empaths, and how they can affect the practice of empathy and communication.

i. Individualism vs. collectivism

This is simply explained as an "for us" mentality as opposed to "for me". While it might sound selfish, individualistic cultures encourage independent thinking and creativity, as well as self-reliance, as opposed to a collectivist culture which encourages harmony through conformity, as well as stronger familial and community ties.

Asian communities tend to be more collectivist, as opposed to Western societies, which tend to lean towards the individualistic end of the scale.

Individuals from collectivist communities may have an easier time training empath skills, due to the ingrained rituals of having to cooperate and prioritize the needs of the many instead of the few, and self. However, as an empath, this may be a problem as well, when wanting to use your empath skills to effect change via unorthodox methods (in your society).

For example - you have gained the trust of a friend who has confided that her husband beats her. A solution would be to divorce him and start anew, or at least live apart. However, in your collectivist society, harmony in the family is a key priority, which means families should live together, regardless of familial violence. Getting her to live apart from her abusive husband then, would be an issue.

How issues like these can be overcome would be to adapt the solution to the culture. If, she is unwilling, you could ask her to get another family member to intervene and live with them to ensure the abuse stops. Not an ideal solution, but a solution nonetheless.

ii. Power distance index

Power distance in essence refers to the extent to which the less powerful members of organizations and institutions (like the family) accept and expect that power is distributed unequally."

In this dimension, inequality and power is perceived from the followers, or the lower level. A higher degree of the Index indicates that hierarchy is clearly established and executed in society, without doubt or reason. A lower degree of the Index signifies that people question authority and attempt to distribute power.

In short - how a culture accepts unequal distribution of power and how strictly rules of hierarchy is enforced in society.

How this affects empaths is that higher degrees of power distance make it harder to effectively communicate and empathize with someone, especially if they are higher up in the social hierarchy than you.

Example: You want to find out what's troubling your boss. Your boss in Japanese. He comes from a culture of high power distance where hierarchy is strictly followed and its rules enforced. The boss doesn't share personal details or about his personal life with his colleagues, or workers.

That's going to be hard as your boss will likely not want to open up to you.

Empath

iii. Masculinity vs. femininity

Masculinity in this dimension refers to "a preference in society for achievement, heroism, assertiveness and material rewards for success."

Femininity however, represents "a preference for cooperation, modesty, caring for the weak and quality of life."

This may have a smaller impact on empaths, however, it is easier to use your empath skills in a culture that is more feminine by nature as compared to masculine by nature, assertiveness may lead to it being harder to suggest or listen to another for both the empath and the subject.

Empathy VS Sympathy

Empathy is very different from sympathy, again.

Empathy is

1. The ability to listen.

2. The ability to reconstruct the feeling of another and reproduce it in a different context.

3. The ability to put yourself into the situation of another.

4. The ability to relate to how others are feeling.

Sympathy is

1. The feeling of sorrow at another's loss or hurt.

2. The formal expression of sadness towards someone.

3. The feeling of pity towards someone to a lesser degree.

4. A shared feeling of sadness, or grief.

In short - empathy is NOT sympathy. You need to draw the line between the two very clearly.

The reason for this, is that as an empath, it can be very easy to be easily drawn into feelings of pity or sadness for another when listening to their account. However, to get the best out of the situation for everyone, you need to understand emotions, their effect, how they affect the person or subject, and how to utilize them for the best outcome for everyone.

That's not to say you can't feel sorry for someone! Or happy, or fall in love, just make sure that you keep your decisions using your empath skills separate, unless those were your aims.

Keep in mind as well - using your empath skills to achieve a vastly unquantifiable goal without any clear metrics may be frustrating.

For example: I want this person to be happy.

How? What is his or her happiness defined by? When will you stop? Will you be encouraging or discouraging them when they do something that runs counter to that goal? The list of questions goes on and on...

Exceptions to the rule (sociopaths and psychopaths)

Exceptions to the rule, of people who employ empathy and empath skills effectively, or lack it, are two groups of people we regularly group together, but in reality are far apart.

Empath

Sociopaths have been theorized to be able to turn empathy on and off very easily, and employ them for self-centered purposes - which makes them highly competent but unethical empaths, which is also due to their excessive practice in socializing, understanding how society works, and a general understanding of human behavior. This, they use to great personal gain, but still blending into society and in fact, influencing and manipulation it to a great degree.

Examples of sociopaths also include lawyers, businessmen, politicians, and other jobs that require high degrees of socializing and the willingness of others to cooperate for desired outcomes.

Psychopaths on the other hand, have been theorized to lack empathy completely, and thus are well known for disregarding the feelings and opinions of others to achieve their own aims, regardless of ethics, morals, and socially acceptable norms.

Chapter 2:

Assess

Chapter 2 covers various aspects of being an empath in practice, as well as certain issues that might hinder or aid you in your life as an empath. Do remember that social situations are constantly evolving, as well as relationships between people. Communication is a dynamic two way process, and as an empath, it is easier and simpler to use your skills with someone in a solo setting, as compared to a crowd, or in a group.

The reason for this, is that although people might feel comfortable with you, they might not be with the social situation or setting that you are attempting to speak to them in.

Empathy and Communication

Being an empath will require you to understand that communication and empathy go hand in hand. A good communicator, does not necessarily need to be a good empath. A good communicator understands how to send and receive messaged efficiently, and clearly, and receive them efficiently and clearly as well.

However, that does not mean that a good communicator is a good empath. A good communicator may know how to speak the lingo and understand how the other person feels to communicate effectively, but lack the tools to encourage the person, allow the person to open up, and take actions that will lead to a best possible outcome for the both of them.

However - being a good communicator is a great place to start.

Good communicators know how to:

    i.   Listen in on details of personal significance from the person

    ii.   Articulate clearly on messages (be they non-verbal, or implied)

    iii. Clarify with the person on unclear messages

    iv. Empathize with the person

Empaths take a few steps further, by understanding that:

    i.   Not all people are necessarily helpful to the empath, or want the best possible outcome

    ii.   The easiest, and best possible outcome may be a bitter pill to swallow

    iii. The best outcome is one where everyone finds a solution that is palatable, and feasible

    iv. Manipulation is not the answer, guidance is, and the difference between both.

    v.   Self-awareness is vital - understanding how others view them is important when gaining trust and relating to someone.

Noise in communication

Noise in communication is another factor that may hinder both empaths and subjects that the empath is speaking with. Noise, is basically any factor that interrupts, or changes the mood, flow, and perceptions within and without, mentally, and physically.

Physical Noise

Physical noise, is basically a dimension of noise that interrupts anyone's ability to communicate clearly and effectively from a physiological standpoint. What does this mean? Anything to do with your bodily functions that may affect the person you are communication to, or yourself, is physical noise.

Examples:

    i.   Fatigue (physical and mental)
   ii.   Hunger
  iii.   Illness

Generally, physical noise is one of the easiest to avoid as long as you catch a persona t the right place and time, as well as assessing what they've been doing, and how they are feeling (physically) by observing their physical appearance.

Take note - make up does wonders for everyone, and can conceal fatigue, as well as illness. To overcome hunger, perhaps offer someone a snack, or invite them out for lunch as well.

Psychological Noise

Psychological noise covers a wide aspect of noise, and is the main body of obstacles in clear and effective communication.

Empath

Psychological noise include biases, pre-conceived notions, cultural influences on perceptions and behavior, as well as strong emotions or the lack thereof. A major obstacle to overcome to become an empath is apathy or as summed up "Empathy needs to overcome apathy for an empath to work".

Anger, sadness, euphoria, as well as boredom, these are all forms of psychological noise as well, if they color your speech and actions, or effect your message to your subject as they are feeling these.

An example would be you trying to find out why someone did something seemingly out of character, however, the person seems to be tired, as well as unwilling to talk, and possibly hasn't eaten in 12 hours.

There are multiple approaches to solving the 2 forms of noise here. Physical noise - hunger and tiredness, as well as mental fatigue. Psychological noise - your own assumptions as to why the person has acted out in a seemingly uncharacteristic fashion, as well as any intense emotion that the person might be having. You need to probe carefully to find out why they are feeling the way they are, while expressing a message of care and concern.

Environmental Noise

Environmental noise is simply nose that comes from the environment around you, as an external factor outside your locus of control. This kind of sound basically provides physical stimuli to your five senses and may transfer into physical or psychological noise later on. Loud noises, smells, sights, heat and temperature, and unusual tastes are all forms of environmental noise

Understand that this kind of noise, while it has a very clear path to neutralize, may not be possible in certain situations. However, the best way to neutralize such noise may be to shift yourself and the person physically to another location with less physical noise.

For example, you are in a crowded bar speaking to someone who just got there. The level of sound coming from other people talking, cheering, toasting, the television on the wall, orders being shouted, the smell of alcohol and cigarettes, the strong taste of a poorly made negroni cocktail, all these affect your message, and your ability to listen to the person.

Thus, by inviting the person to somewhere quieter, with less environmental noise might be a prudent measure to consider. A well-lit park, for example.

Semantic Noise

Semantic noise is basically noise that has to deal with language. Using acronyms, technical language, words not commonly used or understood, having an accent, using regional or foreign languages are all forms of semantic noise that hinder you getting your message across, or receiving and interpreting it correctly.

To counter semantic noise, use clear, concise, and commonly used words. To transmit ideas, try to present them in your simplest form that a 12 year old would understand, without being overly condescending with your tone or language.

For example, you want to tell someone that their job is making them unhappy.

Empath

Would you say: "the conditions of your employment may be the prime cause of your unhappiness"?

OR

"Your job is making you quite unhappy"?

Both carry the same message, one is more complex. Depending on whom you are speaking to, either are appropriate. Make sure to tailor your message for your audience.

That said, usually, the simpler it is, the better. Less room for confusion with 'big' words.

Cultural knowledge (what do you know about their culture?)

In a homogenous culture, your knowledge of what is acceptable within your culture and what is into, comes naturally. However, if you live in a multi-cultural city, or area, you have to consider the effects of an individual's culture on the way they communicate, the way they relate to each other, and acceptable topics to talk about.

So remember, culture affects -

1. Acceptable topics to broach

2. Physical distance between opposite sexes

3. Hand gestures, head gestures, facial gestures (body language)

4. How people relate to each other, over food? Over social events? Solo talking?

Keep in mind that while it may be easier to talk to people in certain cultures, it may not be as easy for them to open up to you due to the level of trust and time. For example, in Asia, it is more common to bond and open up to someone over food and alcohol for employees, friends and family, while, conversely, in certain more conservative countries in the Middle East, apart from alcohol prohibitions, women and men are not allowed to mingle freely, which may be an issue.

The key here, is to understand the person's culture and avoid a faux pas, as well as make them feel more comfortable with your presence and relating to you.

Here's a list of the friendliest cities and countries in the planet:

1. Gothenburg, Sweden

2. Stockholm, Sweden

3. Chicago, USA

4. Boston, USA

5. New York City, USA

6. Copenhagen, Denmark

7. Madrid, Spain

8. Rome, Italy

9. Hamburg, Germany

10. Dublin, Ireland

11. Toronto, Canada

12. Sydney, Australia

Keep in mind that even if you aren't on this list, by observing the local culture and traditions is a good way to start to familiarize yourself with the culture of what is and isn't appropriate.

For example, you want to get to know a colleague better. You take a look at her and realize that she looks Indian, and she speaks to some people on her phone in what seems to be an Asian language.

You need to look closer, listen better, and observe. Without asking her directly, you can definitely gain clues as to which or what culture your colleague comes from.

1. Observe

- What does she eat during lunch?

- A vegetarian diet may indicate that she is a Jain, or perhaps a Buddhist, or perhaps a Hindu.

- A non-vegetarian diet that instead has no pork in it may indicate that she is a Muslim.

- What does she wear, apart from normal office clothing? Are there any personal effects such as amulets, bracelets, or bangles? A round metal bangle worn around the wrist may indicate that she is from the Sikh community.

- What about the clothing? Is it modest?

  This gives you clues about how conservative and potential belief systems, as well as biases or possible prejudice towards certain dress styles (so you know what to avoid dressing like while trying to relate to this person).

- How about social events, does she consume alcohol?

  This may indicate the person's views towards alcohol in social functions, and how trustworthy she views someone who drinks. For some people, drinking together is a shared social event that bonds, for others, it is the antithesis of that.

2. Listen

- What are her opinions on other's sense of dress, and modesty? How about style?

  Similar to looking at her clothing style, it will give you a sense of how conservative she is. To get her to relate o you easily, you might want to adopt a look that she does not feel threatened or offended by. No one ever took a clown seriously, as the saying goes.

- What about her opinions on food?

  While opinions on diet may reveal more about your colleague's demographic, it may not be as telling as what she actually eats. Sometimes, people may contradict themselves to show that what they profess to believe in and actually practice is different.

  Understanding the difference between the two, and showing that you do not judge them for their diet might help them to feel safer and more accepted by you, thus, it is easier to relate.

- Is she well-travelled?

Travelling more, for different purposes can tell a lot about what the person does and likes to do perhaps. Travelling for leisure and the form of travel may indicate perhaps, extroversion, openness to experience and socio-economic status as well.

- Does she speak of visiting parents and grandparents in certain countries?

Travelling for family may indicate a strong connection to a different culture, as most of their family stays overseas, or that they value family highly.

Class knowledge (Socio-economic status)

Socio-economic status ties in with a lot of other factors, especially culture and religion, which also affects beliefs.

Socio-economic status generally just refers to the status accorded to the person by others based off their lifestyle, which is a combination of a few factors listed below. A person's traits and personality, isn't determined by the stars, but by their environment and their guidance growing up.

Age

Age is one quantifier that tells you which generation a person belongs to. While age isn't always accurate, it can help you to roughly gauge how a person would react in different social situations, as well as their health and possible stereotypes they may conform to typical of their generation.

But - remember, while stereotypes are useful, they aren't always accurate.

Gender & Sexuality

Gender is a tricky thing these days. Most people are either biologically male or female. Males have higher amounts of testosterone, and muscle mass as compared to females in general, who have higher amounts of estrogen, and lower muscle mass. Biologically, this may affect the way people react to situations, due to biological factors, such as testosterone causing aggressiveness, or periods causing physical noise.

Apart from that, more importantly, sexuality as identified by a person is a key part of their own identity and how they view themselves. Keep in mind that there is a wide spectrum, and while widely debated, it is best to politely ask the person in question about it, if you are in doubt.

If a spouse or partner is mentioned, asking about, him (male), her (female) or them (pansexual) is usually an easy indicator of the person's sexuality in relation to their romantic partner or interest. Another stereotype is that persons better off socio-economically tend to come out more as LGBTQ due to the lack of other more pressing issues.

Education

Education also determines the rank on the socio-economic ladder. A person inducted into and educated at certain colleges may indicate family wealth and/or ability, as well as a priority on education. A 'good' education does not necessarily indicate that the person has manners, decorum, or is entirely logical, rational and/or objective.

In fact, while an education is beneficial in plenty of ways such as equipping hard skill sets, soft skill sets are socially learned, and these may not be particularly strong as you observe and interact with the person. However, always keep your ears, eyes, and mind open to whatever the person does or says to get a fuller more complex picture.

Certain types of schools may also speak of the persons religious affiliations, such as Catholic or Protestant colleges, madrassahs, convents and so on.

Occupation

A person's occupation, is quite telling of what they do most of the time, and it may make it easier to understand them, as what they do most of the time influences them greatly.

A blue-collar job may also reflect on their education, or their preference. On top of that, does the job need them to be very social? Is it a very hard skill based occupation, or a soft skill based one? These may give you insights into how the person likes to work, and whether they are socially skilled or inept potentially.

In addition to that, working schedules may also inhibit or aid you in getting to know someone better. Night shifts may affect someone adversely, leading to lots of tiredness and other forms of physical noise. A daytime work routine and high stress work environments may also make someone full of mental fatigue, making it difficult for them to focus on you.

Religion/Belief System

Religions or belief systems can offer you a baseline as to the person's morals, beliefs and ethics. Remember, it is just a baseline, and can develop or vary greatly from there on out. Keep in mind, that due to what their belief system is, the person may hold pre-conceived notions of, what you do, who you are and what you are like, if you fit their stereotypes.

Some belief systems may allow a person to be more open and trusting to others, as well as more open to newer ideas, while others do the opposite.

If someone states that they do not have a religion/ belief system, what they mean usually is that they do not follow a fixed set of moral guidelines like those found in formalized religion, e.g. Catholicism, Islam, and so on.

That does not mean that they are amoral or devoid of their own personal set of beliefs, principles and ethics.

A good way to observe and assess would be by asking them harder moral questions that have grey areas, with no fixed outcome. Apart from that, a simple 'what do you believe in?' would be good.

Some people will say

'The inherent good in people'

'Money and power'

'Family'

'God'

As you can tell, some of these answers are not very specific, so you can probe further by asking slightly deeper questions.

'The inherent good in people' - 'Do you think everyone is born well?', 'Is goodness inherent, or cultivated?'

Empath

'Money and power' - 'Does power make one able to help others?', 'Is wealth a sign of the favor of the gods?'

'Family' - 'what is it about family that's so important?', 'Is blood truly thicker?', 'would you adopt?'

And so on, and so forth.

Housing

Housing reveals more about the economic part, than the socio part, although both are represented in this dimension.

The kind of house you stay in, as well as the area that the house is located in, and the general demographic of the area, in relation to the person may give you social clues as to the person's state of finances, as well as their aspirations.

Usually, their childhood home will be the one that impacts them the most, and you can infer the socio-economic class someone grew up in from that.

Do they own their house?

Do they own more than one house?

Do they rent in an upscale area?

What is the cultural demographic in the area that they live?

What about nearby educational institutions?

What kind of industry does their town/city support?

How many people were there in that city or town?

Does it have a unique and distinct culture?

Assets

In essence, the presence of personal owned assets and personal effects may also lend a hand in determining socio-economic status and aspirations. Keep in mind - for both assets, housing, cars, appearances and clothing, all these may inaccurately reflect a person's true socio-economic status, and may be instead an attempt by the person to fit into a different socio-economic class.

For example - ripped jeans and boots are worn by skaters, punk rock fans, metal fans and so on. For British punk rockers, the punk's attire was a reflection of working class Britain, and a blue collar society. In essence, it was what they were used to wearing.

As time went on and their localized culture became a global phenomenon - ripped jeans and boots, as a visual hallmark of punk culture became commercialized, and as a result, now can be bought.

However, it is not a symbol of the blue collar working class - it is a fashion statement and an attempt to fit into that culture by many who now purchase and wear ripped jeans and boots, in a desire to identify as part of the culture and perhaps, socio-economic status.

Conversely, credit card debt can be used to fund more consumerist lifestyles to reflect upper-middle class aspirations and consumption patterns. New phones, new bags, shoes, and so on might also be an attempt to imitate and self-identify as a part of the upper middle socio-economic classes.

Vehicle

Cars and vehicles used are a tricky subject, especially in countries with larger landmasses such as the USA. In larger countries, cars are a necessity for transport due to a lack of public transportation or infrastructure.

However, they may also point to socioeconomic status, based on the type of car, and the taxes, as well as the model of the car. Other vehicles may also provide clues as to the trade that the person plies.

In some landlocked cities such as Singapore, cars are seen as a form of upper-middle class asset, as taxes as well as the purchase prices of cars can be a major part of expenditure and require considerable financial resources to acquire. In addition, the widespread availability and convenience of public transport enables most of the country to not need to use a car.

In Australia however, most of the people that work in a city drives into the city, as they live in spread out suburbs outside of the city limits.

Appearance & Clothing

As with consumer goods, clothing may not only signify socio-economic status, but also cultural affiliation, religious affiliation, as well as sub-cultural affiliation.

The price of clothing and the brand may suggest that the person wants to fit into a certain socio-economic class, or is from that socio-economic class. Dressing up or dressing down may suit your needs, depending on other dimensions in your society.

For example, displays of wealth in some societies, through clothing may be frowned upon as a sign of pride and hubris, while displays of wealth in others are both respected and seen as a mark of success and capability. Thus depending on the society you are in and their perceptions of such dressing, you may want to take into account who you are trying to empathize with and how they will potentially perceive you based off your appearance.

A person may also choose what to wear based off their cultural affiliation, for example, a clear sign is that of a Sikh man wearing a turban. As an empath, you need to correctly identify what kinds of clothing may indicate membership of a certain cultural or ethnic group. Even headscarves and skullcaps have different types, which may lead to you having to change your approach.

For example, you see two men wearing skullcaps, and both are fair, and seem to be of European descent. Naturally, you would assume that they are both Jews, or are they? Even then, within Judaism, there are more liberal and less liberal sections of their society, some of which prohibit them from speaking to women, while others advocate equality of the sexes. The lesson here, is to observe, read up, and brush up on your cultural knowledge.

Sub cultural affinity may also be observed from dressing. Examples of a sub-culture may be, participation in sports clubs, fan clubs for TV series, or games, hobby clubs, or a group of friends with a collective unique identity. The key here as an empath is to identify visual clothing hallmarks of said sub-culture, and then from there on, to understand what are the common factors and activities as well as perhaps, ideologies that they share, or the common binding glue .Once you find that out, it is easier to relate to that individual.

Snap Judgements

Snap judgements of people, while useful, can hinder you in your journey to become an empath and relate to people, as they only offer surface observations as well as information without delving into deeper reasons as to why people act in a certain way or believe in certain things.

In relation to the previous topic, snap judgements can be made quickly by you, but they are also made of you by the person you are trying to communicate to.

What you want, is at best, a good favorable impression made upon the person that you are friendly, and trustworthy, and harmless, but not that you fit into any stereotype or category that they already know to be harmful or untrustworthy. This is because you do not want them to form any biases or pre-judgements of you.

An example of such a character would the kindly old grandfather/grandmother character. Everyone relates to a friendly old man/woman, who seems harmless and dispenses advice. However, a friendly old grandfather or grandmother may actually be someone with ulterior motives, or desires of the person. But, people nonetheless overlook that as they perceive older people to be more harmless and trustworthy in most societies.

You do not want to come off as overly intelligent, pushy, or opinionated when wanting to empathize with someone. You want to be seen as a person that people want to tell their problems to, or share their opinions with as you are highly agreeable, friendly, and open to suggestions. You also want to gain their trust by validating their opinions and actions (regardless of your own actual thoughts and feelings) so as to be able to empathize with them as well as inform and influence them for everyone's best possible outcome.

Body language also plays an extremely important role - learn how to read theirs as well as your own. Crossed arms, eyes looking elsewhere, yawning, and lack of direct eye contact, and lack of nodding to questions, as well as feet pointed away, are all signs of disinterest.

Yours, should be the opposite. Open arms, open hands, smiles, direct eye contact and nodding to their speech as well as facing the person directly should aid you in projecting the image that you are open to their speech. Hugs and cheek kisses upon greeting them for the first time may also be prudent, dependent on the culture and society you are in.

All these will help you to ensure that their snap judgement of you is favorable, while yours should be free of pre-conceived notions, and any notions should be made with proof of actions, words, or patterns that have been proven to be the norm. Even then snap judgments of a person should always be made to change upon receiving more information directly from the person, from people close to the person, as well as from direct observation of the person in work, and social situations.

Asking the Right Questions

Asking questions is for when you want to

1. Initiate contact *(Greetings)*

2. Confirm certain pieces of vital and essential information about your person and subject *(Demographics)*

3. Put your foot in the door mentally and establish a mental image of who you are in the mind of the subject *(Impressions)*

4. Find out where the person stands on personal ideologies *(Ideologies)*

5. Cause the person to question or doubt, or affirm beliefs.

Here are a list of examples.

Greetings

For greetings, you may want to use greetings that are culture specific, especially upon entering an area that is dominated by a culture that is not yours. Be very sure to use the proper terms of greetings, especially for male and female pronouns, and for your position in their society.

If in doubt, always address everyone as your senior, or better. However, it is very much better to ask before going into the situation as to how to use greetings, and what greetings to use.

For example, in Thai culture, the *wai* consists of a slight bow, with the palms pressed together in a prayer-like fashion, and is used to greet seniors, as well as those of a higher or equal status.

In Thai society, if you are a patron, customer, or senior, you do not perform the *wai*.

In some Muslim countries (Islam again, is a religion, not a culture), men are not permitted to shake hands with women, and vice versa, thus, other forms of greeting, such as verbal ones are more appropriate.

Keep in mind that these greetings are the initial point of contact and communication between you and the subject.

Greetings you can use:

1. Hello! (hand wave), and smile

    This is basic, and the most understood worldwide. However, try to use your right hand as most cultures do so.

2. Handshake (Grip firmly, but not till your knuckles or the other's turn white), smile and say hello.

    Keep in mind that certain cultures do not shake hands, and are not welcoming of male and female contact in the form of a handshake. Other cultures such as Thai, Japanese, and Asian cultures are less physical, and while not frowned upon, do not regularly use handshakes as a form of greeting in a non-formal situation.

Demographics

1. You look young, how old are you?

    - This question is used to determine age. As a very basic factor. Do notice that this is targeted towards an older person, as a compliment first, as asking a person's age directly can be seem as blunt and rude.

- For younger children, you can ask what grade they are in, and they might reveal to you their school as well.

2. Is your office in a convenient location? What do you do for work?

- Asking about the location of an office has dual purposes. One, determining the location of an office or workplace may indicate how much the person gets paid. Two, the workplace may not be an office, indicating a different type of profession.

- The second question comes naturally after the first, to make it less blunt. Let the subject speak more and at length if possible so that you may glean more information.

- Some people may start complaining about the job or highlighting aspects that they like, or other concerns.

3. I stay at 'place', where do you stay? Do you want to share a cab?

- You can replace the second question if it suits the situation, and is useful for striking up a conversation while waiting for public transport. If it is someone you are closer to already, you can skip the first question and go straight to the 2nd one.

4. Where do you park your car?

- This is for asking when you want to start a conversation to ask about parking fees, as well as to lead on to learn how much the person pays in parking fees, as well as potentially how expensive their car is. The more expensive a car is, the more likely they park it in guarded carparks in less safe areas of the city.

5. Is that your child/daughter or spouse?

   - This is simply to ask of the person's relation to other people, and might be considered as blunt if you ask it straight up, so make sure you know the person well enough, or at least to be comfortable on a conversational level.

6. I studied at "school", are you an alumni of "school"?

   The first part of the question is to establish a foot in the door, and again, to not make it an interrogative question by offering a part of your life first. Think of it as offering someone a piece of cake when they sit down as an icebreaker.

7. That's a nice cross, is it a cross? (or any other religious/cultural symbol)

   Now, this is a tricky question as some people may either be a bit more shy or embarrassed to share what their beliefs are as compared to less revealing personal information, so this question should be saved for later when the person is more comfortable.

8. Have you tried 'food/restaurant'?

   This is a loaded question - the loaded part comes in which restaurant you choose. The restaurant can be one that has or does not have dietary restrictions, which leads you to finding out if the person has dietary restrictions that may lead to finding out more about their religious or cultural beliefs

Empath

Impressions

Remember that impressions go both ways.

Here, we go through briefly what it means to make an impression, as well as how to manage your image in front of others. Remember - your impression of the subject should not be fixed, and should change based on new information as well as context from other sources.

1. Grooming

Grooming is basic hygiene, as well as looking healthy and smelling good. While there are exceptions to the rule, most of the time, you need to present yourself in your best possible light. People are both more willing, and attracted to others who seem to be in the best physical and mental shape.

- Smell, is extremely important. Pay attention to your body odor, as well as sweat. Make sure to wear fresh clothes daily, as well as to apply a light scent suited to the climate.

- Nails and hair. There is a very clear reason as to why airlines require strict dress codes for their pilots and stewardesses. They need to control the image of their company employees to ensure that you, as a customer or potential customer, will have a positive image of them. And these, go down to the smallest details.

Your nails, should be kept clean at least, and neatly trimmed, or, if suited to the culture or subculture, in line with what is acceptable. For example, black nail polish may be appropriate to certain sub-cultures, but in others, black is seen as a color of death and mourning, and thus taboo.

For both however, healthy nails are definitely regarded better than unkempt ones.

Same goes for hair, covered, uncovered, dyed or undyed, it should be relevant and appropriate to the culture. However, if in doubt, again, keep it neat and short for men, and neat and undyed for women

2. Clothing

In terms of clothing and fashion, when in Rome, do as the Romans do. If in doubt, dress conservatively and without any bright loud colors to attract undue attention. Unless you know that a certain form of dressing or color will help you to feel familiar to the person, refrain from donning bright colors, or patterns that are considered unorthodox.

Keep in mind that countries that have a very wide society with both modern liberal classes and traditional conservative classes, or a mix of both, navigating them might be a bit harder than usual. You need to then understand what role you can play in that society and what kind of character stereotype you want to represent, which we will get to later.

3. Symbols & Signs

For symbols and signs, these are basically items, certain styles of dress, or any identifying marks that identify you as belonging to a certain sub-culture, cultural group, club, association, or nation.

The reason you need to be aware of these signs and symbols you carry on yourself, is that you do not want your subject to have a preconceived notion of you that may or may not be true, or that might put you in a negative light, regardless of your personal affiliations or associations with said culture, sub-culture, and so on.

What you do want, however, is for your symbols, and signs to provide a sense of reassurance through familiarity.

A few examples - wearing a football club jersey that the subject knows or is a member of is one way to establish a common link.

Religious symbols in certain countries may denote a certain class status, or assumption of class status within your subject. In multi-religious countries such as India, it can also denote caste.

A silver cross may denote wealth as the material is expensive, and the cross denotes that you are part of either the Catholic Church or the protestant one. Being a part of a religious class may also denote a higher social status or a wealthier one, as in certain countries, the wide economic divide (economic inequality) mean that most people may have to work 7 days a week, and cannot read or write, thus to be able to partake in religion, need to be educated, and have the time and economic resources to partake in religious ceremonies.

As for subcultures, certain countries have generalized perceptions, such as that all *punks* or football fans of a certain club are violent, or prone to violence. Such symbols or signs would be certain combinations of articles of clothing, haircuts, or explicit club logos.

Keep in mind that certain signs and symbols are not very explicit or obvious, and may involve subtle alterations to dress, such as length of clothing, hairstyle, color, size, and so on. Most clues are visual, while others can be observed by the interactions and of subjects from the same subculture with others outside of the subculture.

Questions you can ask:

1. Why do you wear "insert symbol here"

2. What does the "insert symbol here" mean?

3. Who wears the "insert symbol here"?

4. Where did you get "insert symbol here"?

Ideologies

Do understand that while many people may seem to agree on certain aspects of how to live their lives in homogenous cultures, crafting questions to probe deeper into their psyche also has the twofold effect of gaining someone's trust as well as examining and either re-affirming or questioning what they believe in.

For example - When you ask someone if they believe in an afterlife in a country dominated by a monotheistic religion, you may find out if they are part of the dominant religious group, and if their beliefs are actually in line with what the religion is like, or if they have wondered about it as well.

If they have wondered about it or have doubt, this may indicate several things that you could infer, but mainly a few points:

i. The subject may not be part of the dominant religious group of that country

ii. That subject may not actually believe in the religion

    iii. The subject may be more open to questioning his or her beliefs

    iv. The subject may be prone to questioning what they are told

While none of these may be true, or all of these, but more likely, a combination, remember that the answer to you may also be influenced by what they perceive of you and how you may receive such information.

The most accurate answer would be when they feel safe around you enough to trust you with what they truly think.

What do we look for?

Keep in mind that the human sense are trained to focus on several key factors, as well as influenced by our own forms of experiences and what others have taught us.

When you start to begin to notice things about people, you learn that several categories of things start to pop out at you. Understanding what 'pops' out at you, can also train you to look at smaller, less noticed features, so that you get an accurate picture.

With the sense of sight especially - you tend to notice the most striking features, or features you have been socially conditioned to look out for.

For example - in Tamil culture, upon meeting a lady, the eye naturally observes the forehead to find if the forehead is marked with the status symbol of a married or unmarried woman. As a non-Tamil person, you may notice the bright, vivid and striking colors of the lady's sari (wrapped garment) instead.

Salience

Salience is one of 3 categories in which the human mind directs the senses to selectively receive information. Salience affects things that are personally affective, interesting, or familiar.

Novelty

Novelty deals with how strange, new, or special something feels and looks in a given situation. It can be based off its concept, shape or size. For example - in China, African-Americans are a novelty to the Chinese there, as they rarely see someone of a different skin color.

Novelty might help to spark interest in your subject towards you, as you are different and interesting to them, which might make them open up to you easier.

Familiarity

Familiarity, deals with things that you are familiar with and can identify to, to make you feel comfortable and notice it. When you notice something that you can easily identify and hone into as a hallmark of your cultural or social group, ask yourself - why?

In doing so, you will identify that which is familiar to you, and its source, or role in your life, and psyche. Conversely, you could use items, or personal effects that convey familiarity to your subject to aid them in feeling comfortable around you.

Repetition

Repetition deals with how many times a certain stimuli is shown, and the more times it is shown, the more of a lasting impression it leaves as a result. This is useful in helping people to remember you, and in the future, relate to you as well, as familiarity and repetition go well hand in hand over time.

Just keep in mind that while repetition is useful for good impressions, if you are not making any headway with your subject, repetition will work against you.

Vividness

While salience refers to perceptual cues that make certain things relevant to people, vividness deals with the visual and other sensory qualities of ideas, objects, people, and so on that make them stand out and become very noticeable.

When trying to relate to someone, it can be a double edged sword, depending on the situation and culture. For example, people always notice red cars, but red cars have a higher insurance premium due to the recklessness or perceived recklessness of the drivers.

Intensity

Intensity deals with bright colors, loud sounds, flashing lights, or stimuli that have deep and strong effects on emotions of you or your subject. Again, intensity can work to or against your favor. For example, some people might find deep rumbling belly laughter very enjoyable to hear, while others might be scared off. A bright red dress might attract attention, but also at the same time be inappropriate for a funeral.

Keep that in mind when choosing environments to deal with your subject, as well as the garb you may choose to don when trying to empathize with your subject.

Size

Size is a visual effect that is both easily noticeable, yet overlooked. Size is usually a complement to other factors, but keep in mind that extremes in sizes always attract attention. We never notice the average sized person, we always notice the giant in the room, or the potential dwarf. And again, size is relative. If you're an average sized person in Denmark, you will be big in Japan.

Motion

The human eye (and sense of sight) has been trained to watch for motion. It's a leftover instinct from our hunter gather days. We look for moving things and objects as both opportunity and danger. As such, when trying to relate to your subject, if trying to catch or maintain attention, motion is a useful tool to have. The lack of motion, or slow, subdued motion on the other hand, will likely reduce the threat level that may be perceived by your subject, if he or she is jittery and/or easily frightened.

Figure & Ground

Figure and ground is basically the propensity to observe and engage with the most prominent figure due to the contrast of its surroundings. This can be both visually, or with other senses, as well as mentally. For example - a person holding an umbrella in a crowd, or the first thing you said to your subject that made an impact. All these form perceptions.

They may form perceptions due to the surrounding situation and context, whereas in other situations they may be very normal.

Observing Good Empaths

Their traits, skills, and characteristics.

Keeping in mind the factors that affect both you and your subject - asking the right questions to get information you need is one part of three. The other two parts are gaining trust, and effecting change.

Sometimes, you might not want to effect change, and you might just need information. However, you need to understand that gaining trust is always effective and usually, the first step towards the other 2.

Why then did we tell you how to ask questions first?

The skills needed to effectively look out for clues as to what to ask, also will tell you what kind of person they most likely will be. In that vein, you need to put aside certain biases and frames of minds that you have that will affect your view of them, and help you to empathize with them as a person, and thus, gain trust.

A simple way to get a new view of a person to learn to empathize with them, is to throw out everything you know about them or think that they are, and start afresh. Instead of asking about the **what**, e.g. What are they wearing, what are they doing, what color is their skin, what language are they speaking, what is their religion; ask - **why**?

Why are they acting that way? Why do they eat the food they do? Why are they dressed in a particular manner, and why is it different? Why are they speaking in a particular dialect or language with certain groups of people? Why do they hold this set of beliefs?

When you learn to use the what's to start asking the why's, you'll get a lot more detailed, complex answers that gives you more material to work with, to empathize with someone.

Good empaths can identify ***personal:***

1. Stereotypes

Stereotypes can be useful - but not for an empath when you are trying to get to know a person better. Stereotypes are basically, simplistic views of a category into which a person fits into. For example - all brown skinned Asians are Indians, and like curry. They can get worse from here, and I'm sure you know what I mean. Certain stereotypes of course, are racist, sexist, so on and so forth.

Make sure to re-examine all stereotypes you have, even those that seem relatively harmless and socially acceptable, such as 'all old ladies are polite and kind'.

2. Prototypes

Prototypes are similar to stereotypes, with the difference that while stereotypes may be about simplistic traits, and prototypes deal with the ideal state or ideal form of a person. You may apply it to someone based off a few qualities or things that they do or fit into your prototype. However, most of the time people don't always fit these prototypes.

Keep this in mind - people may have a prototype, and fit you into that, which might make it substantially easier or harder to gain their trust, but it needs careful management of your image so as not to break their perception of you in that prototype.

Conversely, you should try to avoid putting people into prototypes.

Empath

3. Personal Constructs

Personal constructs are simply a set of beliefs that govern our everyday lives. For example - where do we draw the line between animals that are for food, and for pets? Why? Cows, chickens, dogs, cats, rabbits, why do some people eat all of the animals, and some people only eat some?

While this is a simplistic explanation, sometimes, re-examining personal constructs of your subject might give you an in depth look into why they are who they are, as personal constructs are an inventory of their beliefs.

4. Forms of Closure and Need for Closure (Assumptions)

Closure, is simply put, the need to end or finish something. A sentence, an idea, a perception, and so on. The mind does not like blank spaces, so it makes up things, and draws from other experiences and memories to 'close' and form a complete sentence, idea, or memory even.

This should be avoided on your end, and avoided when you are trying to make an impression on your subject, unless it is deliberate.

5. Scripts

Scripts are sets of subroutines and behaviors that we have been socially conditioned to do and understand. While they're useful, it is also worth understanding why this subroutine exists, in the context of a social situation to garner clues as to your subjects' role or place in social settings, as well as the way they behave.

Examples of a script between two people who work in the same building waiting for the elevator after lunch:

Person A: Good Afternoon, how's your day going?

Person B: Good, how about you?

Person A: Great, thanks!

You would not expect Person B to actually speak about how his day actually went, and you would expect him to return the question as well. That's a script.

Scripts are useful in social situations to maintain harmony, or to promote and instill certain values within a community. For example, bows, handshakes, and greetings such as 'peace be upon you', with a reply, 'and peace be upon you too' are meant to show courtesy as well as an expression of goodwill between the two greeters.

Empathy Skill Subsets and Routines

When practicing empathy, remember, as mentioned earlier, empathy comes from within you, as well as without. Through observation and intelligent deduction, as well as asking the right questions, you can get more detailed view of a person, and from there, how to empathize with them.

Here are some things you can do to improve -

1. Journaling

Writing down your experiences from the earliest age you can remember.

- The purpose for this, is to promote self-awareness of how you became the person you were right now. Leave nothing important out. Even if the experiences are negative, put them in. However, make sure you have both positive, neutral and negative experiences that you think helped shape who you were.

- You may realize that at some point, memory gets fuzzy. That's fine. Remember - if you can't recall, don't try too hard, or you might use closure to fill in the black spaces, leading to an inaccurate picture.

- You don't need to write down all the mundane items, e.g. 'I ate a box of cereal each week', unless, it has a point to your development as a character, such as:

"I used to eat a box of cereal every week, it was plain cornflakes, bulk value when I was a kid. I remember asking my mom why I couldn't have *Froot Loops* and she said "that's for rich kids, Johnny, and we're not rich". Now, I still prefer plain cornflakes.

After reading the statement above, what ideas do you have about this person, and what assumptions did you make?

To list a few:

i.   Johnny was what his mother called (him)

ii. He still eats plain cornflakes (why?)

iii. Was he born poor?

Now, imagine, you are Johnny, and write down your thoughts about who you are. Identify the parts in which you use to identify the experiences that shaped you to become the person you are, the hows and the whys are especially important.

2. Immersion

Immersing yourself in a completely new situation

This will take some time and preparation, in terms of event planning. The purpose of this practice is to hone your observation and empathic skills in a rapid-fire, quick response manner.

You need to find a completely new social situation to immerse yourself in with no one or 1 person you know, and the aim is to talk to as many people as possible, and get along with them as much as possible within a stipulated time frame.

Try to pick situations where most of the people know each other to some degree, but are not completely close and well known to each other. A bad example would be a close kit family, where everyone knows everything about everyone and gets along.

A good example would be a hobby club with members from the same town, but from different walks of life.

The goal here is to absorb information, observe their quirks, habits, and preferences, as well as work out what their relationships to each other are. You'll find that you'll make plenty of mistakes. That's good. It takes a long learning process to adapt to a new environment.

    i.   Talk to people, establish their roles and relationships together, to each other

   ii.   Identify a subject you can empathize with the easiest

 iii.   Identify a subject who you think is the hardest to empathize with

 iv.   Identify someone who knows both of them, or who knows about everyone and their relationships with each other, preferably a natural empath or a conscious empath.

    v. Self-reflect on your assumptions and your findings

    vi. Identify biases and effects of other preconceived notions

    vii. Re-examine your findings and assumptions

    viii. Check your findings and assumptions with the person from point iv (empath)

    ix. Reflect on what your pre-conceived notions were, and any other external factors which you had assumed incorrectly or things you had missed out on when you were doing your findings

    x. Repeat process.

3. Reflection

Getting a person, or group of people to tell you, objectively, your flaws.

The purpose of this exercise, when done with a master empath or an empath better than you, will improve your subset skills, as well as scripts. It will help you to seem more approachable, as well as more socially adept with experience.

It comes in two parts - self-reflection, as well as group or individual improvement.

Under reflection - you write down the things you have

    i. Done

    ii. Felt

    iii. Felt like doing but didn't do, and why

iv. Felt like doing and did do, and why

v. Things you didn't feel like doing that you did (that are not necessary for your survival)

- survival needs also include your job, which are work that lies within your defined scope of responsibility)

- For example, you are a clerk. Your job is to type up reports the boss gives you. You mildly dislike it due to its monotonous and tedious nature, but you still do extra few reports for a colleague. Why?

- Why did you go to the gym, or to the church?

vi. Ask yourself all the whys. Why did you do all those things?

The purpose for all these are to examine your own personal values as well as self-beliefs. Once you've got down all these reason, start writing them down. You'll find that this is part of your identity.

You should understand however, that this is part of a matrix of self-awareness.

There are four sections to this matrix. Things you know about yourself that you know, things you know about yourself that you don't know, things about yourself that you know, but other's don't, and things that you don't know, or are not aware of, about yourself, but others do.

This model is simply called the Johari window. Used by psychologists, marketers, and leaders alike, it is used to identify self traits, characteristics, strengths and flaws.

Empath

Using the Johari window is a useful model to understand what you know about yourself first, followed by things you don't know about yourself - how brave you are, for instance, or how hard you can work sometimes, or the limits of your mental endurance in stressful social situations.

However, gathering feedback from individuals and groups on how they perceive you will also be a useful way to ascertain how others view you, as well as previously undiscovered elements that make up your identity. In doing so, you will gain a better understanding of the image you present to others, and make it easier to adapt, modify, and empathize with others by making yourself more approachable in your own mind, as well as superficially to others.

The way to go about this is to find yourself a core or group of people that don't have a bias towards you, and immerse yourself in their social activities before you ask them questions.

Like the saying goes – find people that don't care enough to lie to you, so you can get the objective truth of how they feel.

Things you should be asking them about, are

    i.   How approachable you look

   ii. How approachable you were when they saw you/ heard you introducing yourself

  iii. Their first impression before speaking to you

  iv. Their first impression after speaking to you

   v. What stereotypes did they have of you?

vi. What pre-conceived notions did they have of you and why?

Getting all of these answers, and building up a list will enable you to understand how others see you.

Keep in mind that you should not focus exclusively on one group of people, but instead, several different groups in different subcultures to understand their perceptions of you.

Identifying problems that cannot be solved through empathy

Understanding how empathy works and how you can use it effectively to effect change is good and all, but you need to also recognize your limitations as well as issues that cannot be solved through empathy.

Remember that as an empath, you can use your abilities to hone your understanding of emotions and the way they affect people, as well as effect change, through willing co-operation. However, external forces outside you and your subject's locus of control may play a greater role in determining whether you can affect change or not as well.

Abuse (physical and mental)

Physical abuse should be reported immediately to relevant authorities if possible, and a concrete solution for the abused person(s) should be formed before the relevant authorities are informed.

In any instance of physical abuse, your role should be to firstly:

i. Convince the abused person that they are being abused

ii. Convince them to seek help or accept help from authorities

iii. Formulate a plan for help for the abused to stay away from the abuser

For mental abuse, where the victim is less likely to show visible signs, there are less concrete options or help from authorities, realistically, especially if the abuser is a family member or trusted person from their social circle.

However, mental abuse can be deadly as well, and should not be taken lightly. You should follow steps i – iii above as well, if possible.

Illness

Illness, especially recurring conditions and terminal ones, can really wreck one's psyche, especially when a person has been living with it for so long that it has affected their character and sense of self in a distorted or exaggerated form.

It can be especially hard to empathize with someone if you do not share the same condition, however, when you are able to do so – try to effect change in a way that is both realistic yet positive.

You cannot change a person's illness, but you might be able to change their outlook and how they view themselves, even with the illness.

Mental Conditions

Mental conditions are tricky and best left to professionals – you should not attempt to counsel or effect change in most conditions, and only listen to what the person has to say. Unless you are a certified mental health professional or counsellor, you might do more harm than good.

Beware, while people with mental conditions do benefit and need empathy as well as other emotional fulfilment, their conditions may leave them unable to effect change or be a positive force without proper treatment and counselling, which is again, best left to professionals.

Physical disability

Physical disability is usually very obvious and visible, unless it is something minor, or not very visible, such as dyslexia. Most people with physical disabilities think and view the self differently, and have a different set of problems as compared to able bodied people.

However, talking to them will be a very interesting exercise into seeing how they view you as an able bodied person and your challenges, in contrast to their challenges and perception of self.

Finding your role in your social circle as an empath.

Look back to the cultural values for references to understand your own role in your culture and social setting.

Once you've ascertained your own role and position in your social circle, always try to not be in a role of power, or higher authority, as in all cultures, except those with a low power distance(and even those too). The reason for this, is that in a position of authority, people expect you to be able to effect change for them.

Empath

Remember that as an empath, you need to observe and understand people without them having too many expectations of you so that you get a true look at the different facets of their identity, their perception of self, and reason for doing the things they do, both conscious and unconscious.

Once you've established your role as a trustworthy, relatable insider without any insidious intentions, you can begin. Remember that in your role – you need to maintain your credibility and trustworthiness as well without becoming embroiled in conflicts that may occur within your social circles.

While this may seem easier said than done, understand that you can start by not making promises to anyone, as well as spending time with all the different groups and factions without getting attached to any single one in particular. If you need companionship, try to have it outside of the social circle that you are an empath in.

That said, the more you practice your empath skills, the more you will find that it becomes a part of you and comes naturally. However, avoid being run into a routine or into a set way of thinking by exposing yourself to new situations, people, and groups, as well as being mindful of the company you keep, as well as your assumptions and thoughts in general.

Chapter 3:

Hone

Chapter three is a continuation of chapter 2 - now that you have mastered or at least become more self-aware and able to control and understand how you are perceived, as well as how you want to be perceived and the factors affecting such perception; understanding things that are beyond your control is vital as well.

Understanding your limitations

Physical Limitations

Your limitations are both physical, as well as mental. Apart from your character limitations as established (in the MBTI section) and further explored in the previous chapter under the Johari window, you need to identify potential barriers to your development that are both physical, and outside you locus of control, as well as mental, within your locus of control.

The physical barriers are very simple to identify, yet complex to overcome, or adapt to. For example, you live in a small town of under 300 people where everyone knows everybody. You have an internet connection to seek new knowledge, but you have no one new to meet and learn from. Most people are from the same conservative background with similar values that you grew up in. You're an insider in your community, and it is mostly homogenous, with not much variation in customs or culture.

You want to improve your cultural knowledge, as well as meet new people and sub-cultures to learn from them. To do this, you need to make enough cash to get out of town to meet new people, as well as to shift out of your hometown. On top of that, you'll need to pay off your housing mortgage and maintain your family's expenses too. Not very possible in the short term is it? That's a physical limitation.

Identifying such limitations is the first step to understanding and then overcoming then. Sure, you could use the internet to learn about new cultures, Skype with people from elsewhere, but that's it. You'll need real life experiences and to immerse yourself in new situations to develop.

Psychological limitations

Psychological limitations, apart from cognitive biases identified in the earlier chapter, deal with mental scars, or fears that you might need to overcome, as well as other lacking qualities you may have, such as lack of confidence, anxiety and so on.

While some of these may be legitimate mental conditions which you may need therapy and counselling for, if it is not - you may need to overcome them gradually by identifying them first.

It may 'all be in your head' but it definitely affects how you view the world and react to it. It definitely also affects your mental self- awareness and perception of self, so do take note of that.

While counselling is effective, so are other practices such as meditation, as well as the best treatment of all, gradual improvement through experience. Accepting that you will fail, and screw up immensely over time will help you to lower your own expectations of self, and then followed by self-reflection, and learning, you will get better and overcome mental limitations.

How to overcome your areas of weakness

As mentioned in the previous section, overcoming your own weaknesses requires you to correctly identify them.

The issue with this is that all too often, we cannot identify our flaws on our own. Cue the Johari window. After you've done that, make sure you keep a close friend who can help you to keep track of your progress in becoming a better, more self-aware, socially competent empath.

On top of that, practicing mindfulness, and building your willpower is essential.

However, this can only happen if you take care of yourself. Physical and mental health come into play for this. Make sure that you self-care appropriately by following the basic hierarchy of needs.

- Get 8 hours of sleep

- Exercise

- Eat healthily

- Get enough sunshine

- Maintain healthy relationships with people around you

- Reserve enough time for passion projects

Empath

- Find fulfilment in your everyday life
- Get enough time to self- reflect and think through your day

Identifying factors and people in your social circle who prevent you from becoming an empath

As an empath- you encounter a few types of people who either leech off your energy and time, or prevent you from becoming better directly by pushing you down and belittling you. You need to let go of these kinds of people to be able to help yourself focus on becoming a better empath, without which it will be a lot harder and nigh impossible at times.

You can do this in several ways - by shifting yourself physically away, or by cutting off contact and awareness of these people. Social media, is especially potent. Unfollowing such people and blocking them from your social media accounts as well as informing your friends that you are finished with being their associates, while it may sound harsh, will benefit you in the long run.

Learn how to identify them.

Toxic people

Toxic people generally deny that things happen to them because of their actions, and place the responsibility for their faults and problems on the shoulders of others.

In addition, they may also display abusive behavior and language, such as name-calling, aggression, toxic masculinity and feminism, 'friendly' insults, gossiping, incessant lying, and emotional manipulation. These people are best left to develop on their own, instead of you having to deal with them.

Remember that even if you are trying to help them, it requires them to recognize that they have a problem and take concrete steps to change. If they do not, they are just lying and manipulating you for friendship, or what they can gain out of your friendship with them.

Prototype expectations

Prototype expectations are slightly different. Instead of them affecting you, prototypes, as mentioned earlier are the ideal version of someone imagined by you. This is mainly you, but the easiest way to draw free of their influence and prevent yourself from idolizing them and their existence is to cut them off, or to stop being in their orbit to 'discover yourself'.

By discover yourself, I don't mean to go on an eat pray love trip to India or whichever third world country on a spiritual odyssey. What I mean, is to understand how you would react uniquely to different situations and people without the expectation of yourself to live up to this person, real or imagined.

Soul suckers

Soul suckers are the last and also quite unique version of toxic people. While they lack the lying, emotional manipulation and normally identifiable traits of toxic people to be around, they feed off your energy and emotional feedback and validation you deliver to them. Thus, the term, 'soul' suckers.

To identify a soul sucker, look for someone who constantly gripes, moans and complains about their life, themselves, or anything, especially when harping on a particular topic. It could be the death of a loved one, a bad breakup, the loss of a job, or the 'good ol days' even.

They drain you of energy to deal with people by demanding your sympathy and attention constantly, and they also bring your mood down, adding to your negativity and cultivating a negative outlook to life too, in bad scenarios. Keep in mind that you're not being cruel by letting them go, you are improving yourself and giving them a wake-up call.

Conclusion

$\mathbf{N}$ow that you've read through this book, you'll hopefully, become more aware of how to connect to people with empathy.

Remember that being an empath is hard, and being an empath doesn't make you the center of attention, on the contrary in fact.

Always keep an open mind, observe with your eyes, and listen with your heart as well as your ears. Live well.

www.ingramcontent.com/pod-product-compliance
Lightning Source LLC
Chambersburg PA
CBHW060801260726
48660CB00002B/723